RECESSION-PROOF SETUPS

21 Proven Stock Market Trading Strategies In a Bear Market

Matt Giannino

ISBN 978-1-7345540-3-8(softcover)
ISBN 978-1-7345540-1-4(e-book)

Giannino Products and Services
394 Cypress St.
Broomfield, CO 80020
www.marketmovesmatt.com

Contents

Glossary

After-Hours – These are hours after the market closes, during which trading is not open to the general public but a select few. This can cause the price of stock to gap up when the market opens.

Bearish Order – When moving averages are ordered from slowest to fastest, top to bottom. For example, a bearish order could be the 100 moving average on top of the 50 moving average on top of the 10 moving average.

Bullish Order – When moving averages are ordered from fastest to slowest, top to bottom. For example, a bullish order could be the 10 moving average on top of the 50 moving average on top of the 100 moving average.

Bollinger Bands – Bollinger bands show the volatility in a certain stock at any moment; these can also be seen on the stock charts. These bands encapsulate price and expand/contract from volatility. They also are great places to enter or exit trades when prices touch.

Candlestick Patterns – The candlesticks not only tell us what happened that time frame in the market, but they can also tell us what is going on in the big picture. Certain candle formations as well can tell us what exactly will happen tomorrow. Candlesticks are a great place to start learning the market and what the oscillations mean.

Capitulation – This happens at the bottom of selloff or at the top of a bull run and is associated with extreme volume. This is where traders mass liquidate positions at a market top or buy large amounts of shares at the market bottom.

Chopping / Choppy – The movement associated with a market with no direction. This is where the market is range bound and often found to gap up and down consistently. This can be very frustrating for traders trying to nail a direction, but very lucrative for option sellers.

Close – The top of the body of a bullish candle or the bottom of the body of a bearish candle.

Confirmation – This is the exact moment when the trader's bias line up with the market. For example, if a trader thinks that a stock will bounce off a certain price level, he is really guessing until the market gives evidence it will. This evidence of the trader's bias could be that the stock actually starts reversing at that price level. This evidence is called confirmation to the trader.

Consolidation – *Consolidation* is where the market pauses from the direction it has been traveling in. During this pause price is moving up and down, but not really going in a bullish or bearish trend. This *consolidation* can be in the form of a wedge, triangle, or channel. Defined more later in the book. Defined more later in the book in the important terms section.

Day Trader – Someone who enters and exits anything in the market on the same day

Divergence – When the market keeps dropping or popping and the indicator is doing the opposite. This signal tells trader there is likely to be a reversal in the market.

Gaps – (verb) Whenever the market opens higher or lower than where it closed, it produces a gap. A gap can tell a trader a lot whether we will continue higher, fill the gap, and more.

Gaps – (noun) Places in the market where no buying and selling has occurred. Gaps are key pieces of information to understand the market strength or weakness, and there are specific ways to invest and trade from them.

Higher Low – Where the drop of a stock in the market is higher than the previous drop (low).

Long – Where traders believe the market will go up. Being long means, holding positions to profit from this movement higher.

Lower High – Where the pop of a stock in the market is lower than the previous pop (high).

MACD Oscillators – This is another very common indicator that can tell a trader when a trend is reversing or beginning. This indicator has a lot going on, so it is not the easiest for beginning traders, but it certainly is one of the favorites.

Moving Averages – These are lines on the stock market charts that average a certain number of past prices. These are very helpful because they can help users find new support and resistance areas as well as help us gauge current trends. By using these averages, we can learn a lot about the market.

Open – The top of the body of a bearish candle or the bottom of the body of a bullish candle.

Oscillations – This is the act of moving back and forth. For a stock, this could be movements between two different prices. For indicators, this could be movements between two different values.

Oscillators – Types of indicators that move between two values. These indicators could give traders extreme levels for buy or sell signals.

PreMarket – These are hours before the market opens, during which trading is not open to the general public but a select few. This can cause the price of stock to gap up when the market opens.

Price Structure – Amount of buying or selling at certain price levels.

Pullbacks – Short pauses or small reversals. During a large move, or trend in the market, a stock will typically move in the opposite direction shortly after. This short-term move results in a continuation of the trend shortly after. This is how stocks move in a healthy direction.

Retracement – This is a pullback or reversal of a certain percentage. The most popular retracement is 50%. If a stock moves a certain magnitude down, it could reverse half the previous move. Which would be called a 50% retracement. This is ideal for planning profit taking levels.

Risk to Reward – This is where traders find profitability. By planning a trade before hand they can know if it is worthy of taking. This involves knowing what you are risking and what you are trying to make. Any risk to reward above 1:2 preferentially 1:3 is a great set up.

RSI (Relative Strength Index) – One of the most popular indicators. RSI is an oscillator between 0 and 100. Readings around 60-100 are called "overbought" and readings around 0-40 are called "oversold". RSI tells you when the market is a sell or a buy from these extreme readings and is mostly a reversal indicator. Knowing this information can help us enter trades or investments as well as scale-out or exit them.

Scale into A Trade – This is the trading/investing technique for how to properly use position sizes. Scaling is the act of spreading out those orders to achieve the lowest possible average price. You can also scale out of trades, which help you achieve the highest possible exit price.

Smart Money – Money controlled by big banks, institutions, or savvy investors that can manipulate the market because of this amount of money. Traders will regularly follow smart money to ride momentum and avoid getting burned.

Short – Where traders believe the market will go down. Being short means, holding positions to profit from this movement lower. The big concern with being short, is holding short positions, which involve borrowing stock, options, or more. Most brokers will charge a fees for borrowing.

Stop Loss – A place traders will look to exit a position for a loss. This allows traders to avoid larger losses and define how much they are willing to lose in any trade.

Stopped Out – The act of a trader's stop loss getting hit and exiting their position. This can be executed automatically from your broker from an order put in previously.

Straddle – Buying a call option and a put option at the same strike price.

Strangle – Buying a call option and a put option at the different strike prices.

Strong Hands – Shareholders that are quick to hold their shares during any bad news, panic, or fear

Support/Resistance – This is a place in the market where stocks have previously bounced if it happened once in the market, it is likely to happen again. Charting these can give traders/investors great places to enter or exit.

Swing Trader – Someone who enters and exits anything in the market in 1–10 days

Technical Analysis – This is the art of reading stock charts. By analyzing them properly with indicators and patterns, you can get a general edge to help you maximize gains and minimize losses.

Time Frame – Time frames are on a stock chart, just showing the price movement for that time. For example, the 1 minute time frame shows a bunch of 1-minute candles. Each candle represents price movement for one minute in this example. Multiple time frames have different strengths and weaknesses.

Trading Patterns – The stock market gives opportunities for you to draw, triangles, wedges, support, or resistance lines, and with these patterns, you will have the ability to trade or invest from them. For example, if a stock is touching a support line that it has previously bounced off of, that may be a great place to enter a trade.

Trailing Stop Loss– This is where the stop loss rises with the price of the stock. This is a fixed percentage a trader is willing to risk. For example, if the stop loss is set to 5% and the stock rises 10%, the stop loss will be raised to +5%. Meaning the trader will actually lock in positive 5% instead of negative 5%, if the stock reverses.

Triangles – This is a common trading pattern where the stock market may form a triangle. This is a period of consolidation that normally leads to a large breakout.

Volume Profiles – Volume profiles are like daily candle volume but they appear on the horizontally right side of the chart. They can help traders visually see how much buying has occurred at each price level. The more bought, the more resistance or support will be at that price.

Weak Hands – Shareholders that are quick to sell their shares during any bad news, panic, or fear

Wicks – Black lines extending the candle bodies. These indicate weakness in the movement for that candle or trend.

About Market Moves
Matt Giannino

Feel free to skip this part if you don't want to hear how I started trading, I lost it all, quit my job for it, turned accounts from $3,000 to $25,000 multiple times in just a couple of months, teach hundreds how to trade daily, and most importantly found my passion in life. It isn't that exciting.

As you may know, I am or was a professional runner, depending on when you are reading this book. But back in 2016, after my first stress fracture, I used that time to become obsessed with another hobby called Day Trading the Stock Market. For someone working a part-time job that paid very little, this seemed like a dangerous and risky way to spend my free time. I mean, I knew very little to nothing about trading stocks.

One of the main reasons I was attracted to it was a conversation I heard between my Dad and Nick. Back in Boston, after skipping my race that I was too injured to run, they were rambling about the stock market and how everything was 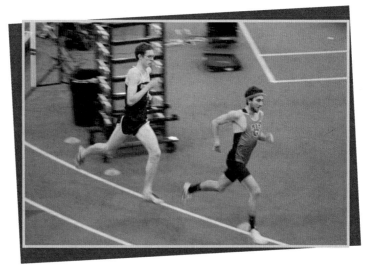 beaten up and had plenty of room to run. This amazed me, seeing my Dad and my best friend Nick so excited and passionate about a subject that I heard very little about. Nick was very interested in playing the stock market every day, while my Dad was giving us advice about investing long term. Everything

I heard perked my ears up and moved some rusty gears in my brain. The rest is really history from that day, I dove into stocks and trading with everything I had (literally). This is very common for me; I have an all in or not in mentality. With all this new free time, I was especially all-in now that I could not run and had to find other ways to make my time productive. Running has really let me down lately, and now is the time to increase my knowledge or skills somewhere else. Always keep growing is my mantra, and if you stop growing, you are dying. It is basically science, I mean what else is the point of this life than to make the most of it. Become a better person every day and consistently throw ourselves into the depths of change. That is what I did.

That cold winter in 2016, I spent almost all my time watching CNBC, going to Barnes and Nobles, reading books, and waiting for myself to heal. It was a dark and wonderful time. I started trading with $3,000. For the first 90 days, I would not have to pay trading fees, so luckily, I was really experimenting in the market. During that time, the market was going up every day, and I could only buy stocks, so I felt like a genius. My portfolio was up 50% easily in the first couple of weeks. How could I not be good at trading when stocks rocketed higher every day. I mean, they were coming off very low levels and finally popping. The fact that I could only go long made it easier for me to make money. Obviously this was not enough; having this early success, I wanted to learn more. I stumbled upon options trading not long after being in the market. Which is possibly one of the riskiest ways to trade the stock market, most options expire (or become) worthless. Which means there were unlimited

ways to lose money. But I loved the fact that I could gain leverage from them. If I picked a trade properly instead of making 3%, I could make 80-100%. Why would I not take the options trade? If you guess it, it did not take long before my impressive gains withered away to nothing. Literally nothing, I ended up losing everything in my portfolio, trading those options. Of course, I did, because I had no rules, no structure. The market has no structure. If you mix those things with no structure, it is bound to end in a total financial loss. So I took some time and rethought my strategy. I tried to understand how much more money I could risk in the market, and then I dove back in.

I just got a couple of paychecks and took a week's breather from trading. I realized my mistakes with these foreign derivatives called option trading and moved on. I think now is the time to restart and try again. Not long after that the same thing happened, I stumbled hard and sent another account to zero. Amazing. During this time of healing my injured body, I am also subjecting myself to financial losses. It was miserable, but I went back to the library and the internet to learn more and more and more. I knew the long term benefit of understanding the stock market, and I didn't want to give up on it. I mean tons of people owe 80,000$ in student loans. I just paid $4,000 to the university of trading. It seemed like a cheaper education, in my opinion. One day, I may have $50,000 or even $1,000,000, and at that point, I may see my portfolio swinging $4,000 a day. Long term, I saw the light, I saw the possibility. I knew that this was chump change compared to what I was going to be doing in the future. So that justified using this money to learning. Money really doesn't mean anything; life is short. I don't want to put much emphasis on being rich. I just want to develop skills, especially skills that can make me financially free.

This has already been a long ramble on my back story to trading. Fast forward to 2019, and everything has changed, everything! Good and bad. I spent the next three years trading the markets on and off. On and off, meaning that I would lose everything, I wait a couple weeks or months, deposit some more, and try again. I attempted trading the markets many many times. Options were really really hard. If you had poor risk management, which I had, it was almost impossible to keep any streak going. 2017 ended with a huge loss on my tax return. 2018 started on a bad note but ended much differently. Obviously my negative momentum in 2017 to 2018 led me to lose some money early in 2018. But once I started investing in the summer in stocks and crypto, everything changed. I started my portfolio out with $12,000, and months later, I found it at $25,000. This return was unreal to me, and my options strategy and crypto strategy was finally working. It felt amazing, and I was really killing it. I was so confident that I found the strategy and my purpose or passion in life, I finally quit my part-time job. This was where I taught after-school engineering class and got paid 40 bucks a day. It took about 3 hours, and I had to manage 10-20 kids playing. This was also my third year with the company, and it was time for a change. I just want to say that I had an amazing time meeting all these co-workers, the job gave me the ultimate freedom (I rarely saw my boss, I was my own boss), and I really did it as a means to give back my knowledge of engineering to kids. 90% of the time, I tried to pour my soul into those classes. Helping those kids learn, be more confident in themselves, and have fun, most importantly. It taught me about teaching people, interacting with kids, and being comfortable managing people. These skills will help me out in 2018-2019 just wait (full circle).

So my confidence in trading and investing led me to quit, buy a huge TV as a monitor, and try full-time trading from home. Yeah, I bet you are cringing right now. It seemed like the universe was leading me, so I listened and followed. The signs were there honestly. Not to mention that right before I quit, I shorted the overall market for the first time right before the biggest pullback in 10 years. Yeah, again, confidence was high....too high. So ended up day trading from home for the first month. In the back of my mind, I knew that this freedom was a little too dangerous, and if not appropriately managed would be bad for me.

The big reason I could trade and have more freedom was that if my account is above $25k, I am allowed to trade AS MUCH AS I WANT. Sorry to not mention that part, so that extra freedom was what I was talking about when I said I need to balance it properly. But like I said before, I have no risk management and no rules. I am still bound to fail in the long run, according to most trading books I read. So all this change and being able to make unlimited trades was also coupled with trying to trade futures. This basically was like starting a fire at the gas stations. I was bound to blow up in the worst way. So futures are a derivative different from options in the sense that your losses are not limited, which means that you could lose way more than you put in. If you think this sounds awful, you are right. Oh yeah, I also didn't mention that because the market dropped the largest amount in the last ten years, this jacked up the volatility to insane levels. This means that you make a lot of money quickly and lose a lot of money quickly. These levels were 1 to 3% moves a day in the index when the average was only under 0.3%. It was the most dangerous time to be investing in futures. But I went right in as I do and tried to learn the good and bad lessons first hand. The first couple of days, good momentum carried my account to 28k. And shortly after that, my account dropped below 25k, which is the threshold you need to have to trade as much as you can. So that was tough and added some pressure to trade my way back above 25k. The market was climbing day by day, and I was holding onto my two futures positions, losing thousands of dollars.

I would wake up every day, and it kept rising. My account was slowly shrinking and under 15k at this point. I was fully expecting the market to drop hard and enter a bear market, the super bear market everyone has been waiting for, but it didn't. Just when I sold all my positions to cut my losses and ended the bleeding, my account was at 13k. Which was almost half of what it was when I started. This was too devastating, so I vowed to stay away from futures and decided to take a break. Shortly after I sold, the market did sell off a large amount, the move I was waiting for. If I held everything, my account would have jumped to 50k. Letting me learn the most obvious lesson, right after you sell, is when your move happens. This happens all the time. During this time of trading, I became a little too obsessed, and it definitely took away from my running. I would not be able to sleep if I held any positions overnight, which cuts down on recovery from training obviously. During this time, I still managed to run a 3:43 1500m and a 1:52 800m personal record in track. Oh yeah, you probably forgot that I was still professionally running, and actually healthy now. So I still could balance both, but I would be lying if I said trading didn't take a toll on running in some way or another.

Fast forward one more time to the latter half of 2018 after getting married. During this time, I started a youtube channel that grew to more than 1,000 subscribers enough to get paid by youtube daily. I can attribute this idea and success to Gary Vee. He is an online influencer who preaches putting content on the internet (DOCUMENTING), which is what I am doing. So I listened to him, and now I have one form of passive income and slowly adding more social channels. My goal is to eventually be an online trading influencer, sharing my skills and trades daily. I started trading on Robinhood because it was a free platform where plenty of millennials went to invest. The youtube search was through the rough for Robinhood videos. It was crazy. So I went to this platform just to dabble in investing and show others how to trade.

Only a month later do I buy options to put on TLRY, while it is climbing to 300 and then in the flash of an eye drops to 150$. It was crazy that I was involved in the most profitable day trade in history, I would say, and I was buying this at the exact top. This jacked up my 3,000$ account up to $12,000. It was mind-blowing. The momentum from that led me to get my account to $25,000. Once again, over the day trading limit. Now I was back in business, and I could trade full time again — no more restrictions.

The freedom was back...but could I handle it? This, in the meantime, was all live on youtube, the trades, and the progress. I was displaying it to the world. I would wake up and show my users how to make $1,000 in 15 minutes. I made a $3k to $50k challenge on youtube and slowly brought my account to $46k!! Every day I woke up, I kept making money, and I saw my account grow in a way I didn't think was possible. I was in the zone. At some points trading, I would stretch a little too far and lose a significant portion, like 5-7k. And have to put myself back in check and be smarter. Then one day, I hit 46k, and I wanted nothing more than to hit 50k in front of all my viewers and complete the challenge. From getting married, running fast, getting my account to 25k twice in one year (almost to 50k), creating a youtube channel, personal brand, and more. It has been wild.

Nowadays, what I spend most of my time on is trading, a big surprise. I also post content on youtube every week, teaching traders everything they need to know, as well as offering free courses on my website. I also learned a valuable lesson after making $40,000 in 2 months, that money without people is lonely. It sucks. That is why I share my options trades and setups with a premium trading group every week. This is the best of all worlds; I can trade, teach, and connect with some amazing people. I would love to buy you seven days into my group, no cost for you.

Just click the link here: https://www.marketmovesmatt.com/trade-alert-special

The Power of This Book

If you read my backstory, you may have figured out I spent way too many hours staring at a computer screen watching candlesticks tick up and down. Many people would have given up after going through what I went through, but not me. I never gave up, and I entered the University of Trading every single day of the week. Paid my tuition, learned my lessons, you name it. During these crazy years and 10,000+ hours, I noticed the way the market moves that not many people could ever see. This is where you come in, every pattern, trick, consistency, I saw is logged in this book. These patterns, I learned the hard way, and if I knew them when I first started, my account would be looking a lot different. I put in the screen time till my eyes watered to find secrets in the market that I want to give to you. These are going to be in the form of the very finest setups I have ever spotted trading the stock market professionally for 10,000+ hours. I hope you understand the value and potential of this book, and I hope you take it seriously.

Tips to Success

Bear Market / Recession

Bear market and recession is a term used with huge consistent selling in the market. During these times the market will fall for multiple months and companies will start missing earnings. It is a very scary time to be an investor but a very exciting time to be a trader. In this book, all setups are geared towards bear markets or recessions. Which means we are trying to make money on the big drops in the market. There is plenty of opportunity in buying the bounces, but just know it can be extremely dangerous and those trades should not be held long. This is because, as traders, our goal is to go with the direction the market (selling), so we will focus more on the short entry points. Bear markets can be the easiest to trade, because it provides traders with volatility. If you look at every recession, volatility was sky high, which makes trading extremely easy and lucrative. Traders just need to know what to look for! I do believe the setups in this book could really open your eyes to those opportunities.

Study the Book

Here is the thing, this book has setups that I have found to work time and time again. For any new trader, you will read this book, see the setups, and maybe only remember one or two when the market is actually moving in real-time. That is okay! These setups took me years to actually spot instantly charting or trading. The only way you will be able to spot these instantly is by keeping this book by your computer or nightstand and pulling it out every night. The whole goal is cementing these charts in your brain, so when the market moves, it is almost like second nature to say "Double bottom" let's get in on channel breakdown; let's play the drop! Great things take time. Just think about a baseball player hitting a fastball in a split second. They didn't get that ability overnight; it took years of training their hand-eye coordination, reaction time, and form. This book is your training and will help you react faster and more intelligently. This won't happen if you read this once and put it down. Training takes years, and if you want to be good at trading, you need to be consistent and do the hard things.

Ride Momentum and Nailing Pullbacks

You will notice a common theme throughout the book, and you may be shocked by how similar all the setups really are. This isn't because I am trying to rip you off or fill the pages; this is because successful traders understand two things riding momentum and nailing *pullbacks*. You can only make money when you have direction, but once the market chooses a direction, what do you do? Get in right away? Probably not, you may get in on false move or at the very moment the move is over. What the best traders all over the world do with market direction is nail the *pullback*. It is tricky, part science, part art. That is what most of these setups attempt to do, help you nail *pullbacks* at a micro-level for a macro move. The worst way to trade is trying to call the exact moment a lengthy trend dies and the market reverses. Every trader since the beginning of time feels this is a good strategy. This produces menial gains for the trader, compared to trading with the large trend. That is why there are only a few reversal setups in this book. The majority of these setups are just different ways of getting into *pullbacks* in the market, different ways of spotting them, and different circumstances for them. So again, if you feel like all the setups look similar, it is because the concept is, but the details are different. Remember, the devil is in the details.

Entering a Trade

All of the setups in this book will contain guidance on how to enter. Traders mostly care about entering short positions when the market is falling hard. Like stated previously, because of the nature of a *bear market*, playing bounces higher can be very lucrative but also very risky. In some setups there will be multiple places to enter, one risky and one safe. There is one reason why it is important to know the risky entry point. Simply put it may produce more profit, so in some cases it may be worth entering there. These risky entries into trades are only for well-seasoned traders who can manage the risk. The risk involved is a less probable place for the trader to profit and an increased chance of getting *stopped out*.

We Need A Strong Trend

As traders we need volatility and trends to give us a higher chance of making profits. The good news is we have volatility and a strong trend in a bear market! The huge selling pressure will produce, large *pullbacks*, long *consolidations*, and a high likelihood, and the trend will continue. Basically, you get a more predictable and sizable movement within the stock. This increases your risk to reward ratio and helps you be more profitable long term. The reason this is true is that if strong trends mean larger moves, traders can make more and risk less with any setup. That is how traders stay in the game the longest by always risking a small amount to make a large return. You may try and use these plays on lower time frames with smaller weaker trends but just know the chance of success greatly diminishes.

Have an Exit Plan

It can't be said enough that when trading the stock market, you need an exit plan. I am not talking about the mouth-watering profit zone, and how many Lamborghinis you will buy when the stock goes there. This is what too many traders do, romanticize the win, and rarely think about the downside. The downside is just as likely to happen as the upside is. So I urge everyone reading this book to plan your trade correctly, which includes a *stop loss* with a profit zone. I just want to make it known that these setups won't help you avoid losses for the rest of the time. Instead, these setups should help you hopefully take less losses over time, but more importantly, to recognize common real-time patterns.

Setting a Stop Loss

Throughout the book this line will be used when referring to a stop loss, "*The amount traders risk is fully dependent on how much they think they can make.*" When planning out a trade, traders will have an idea of how much they can make. For example, they may believe they can make 10%. Knowing this can make it very easy to figure out how much to risk in a trade. Most traders use a risk to reward around 1:2 or 1:3. The higher the risk to reward, the higher the likelihood a trader will be profitable in the long term. Using simple math, if a trader plans on making 10%, they can risk 3-5% depending on the risk reward ratio chosen. This will greatly help plan how much to risk in any one setup.

Time Frames

The key to indicators, patterns, setups, and all technical analysis aspects is using the correct time frame. Or at least having the right expectations for the time frame you may be trading. The general rule and expectation are that the larger time frames you use, the more accurate and consistent technical analysis will be. This means that most of these setups will become less and less accurate, the lower the time frame. The reasoning behind this is simple; if you are looking at the monthly chart, one candle represents 30 days of price movement and volume. You can make the argument that the monthly candle has 30 times more volume than the daily candle, that means a lot. You can also make the argument that a pattern on the monthly time frame or setup on that time frame, is 30 times more likely to move as expected. If a daily candlestick setup had a 1 to 300 chance of moving as expected, the monthly time frame might have a 1 to 10 chance of moving as expected. I hope this opens your eyes to the power of the higher time frames as well as the dangers of the lower time frames. As you move lower and lower, you have less volume and are subject to volatility more easily. So my point is to know the time frame and the expectation and be prepared for less accuracy on the lower time frames for these setups.

Don't Expect Success

Like any tool in life, it may have amazing capabilities and huge potential, but if you don't know the technique, you won't see the fruits of your labor. The same thing with the skills you learn in the stock market and technique just comes down to execution and emotional control. Any setup you learn in this book might have the potential to be a clear winner all the time, but that is only 50% of the equation for success. The other half comes down to entering the trade, exiting, added to the position, taking off, honoring your stop loss, or profit zone. As you can see, the problem generally doesn't lie in setup but really lies with your choices. Execution is a make or break for a trader, but I am not here to scare you away from trading. My main goal is to provide you with every edge you can possibly have. If the equation for success is setups and execution, then taking the setups out of the equation will make your job much easier. If you can perfect your execution there is no doubt in my mind you can move the markets like a magician.

Important Terms

I am going to go ahead and define the most important terms in this book. If you don't read these terms and fully understand them, this book might be another language. So please, just know these terms before diving into the setups.

Trend

We will be discussing this term in every single setup. A trend is simply a time in the market where the stock is continually moving in one direction. A bullish trend is one where the market keeps making new highs, AKA going higher. A bearish trend is one where the market keeps making new lows, AKA going lower. The more highs or lows the market makes, the stronger the trend. Like going up a flight of stairs, one step at a time, you go higher and higher.

Consolidation

This is another term we will be discussing in every single setup. *Consolidation* is where the market pauses from the direction it has been traveling in. During this pause price is moving up and down, but not really going in a bullish or bearish trend. This *consolidation* can be in the form of a wedge, triangle, or channel. This is a period where buyers and sellers are battling for control, and the result is a bearish or bullish trend. This can be seen in the chart above by the channel that has defined *support* and *resistance*. During this time, the market has no direction and is trying to figure out which direction it wants to go. *Consolidation* periods shortly follow a trending period. Like the example above, the first *consolidation* period was followed by a bull run, and the second one was followed by a sell-off. It is hard to know which direction it will be, but with the right setups in the book and clues, you should have a better idea.

Reversal or Pullback

A reversal is exactly what it sounds like, a point in the market where direction changes instantly. For this book, we are only talking about large reversals. Which could be the end of trends or small *pullbacks* from a trend. The difference between a *pullback* and a reversal, is a *pullback* is temporary and allows traders to enter the trend. While a reversal is most likely the end of the trend for some time. *Reversals* last long and become a new trend for the stock. While *pullbacks* are short-lived and can be missed in a blink in some instances. For a bullish trend, a reason for a *pullback* would be an increase in selling pressure or a decrease in buying pressure. Some reasons for this increase in selling pressure could be news driven (Trump tweeting), many sell orders at key price levels (ie. $10, $100, $1000), uncertainty for investors, technical resistance (ie. moving averages), or etc. Obviously most stocks go up over the long haul (5-10 years), so unless the stock has bad fundamentals, the overall direction is always bullish, which means all drops are just *pullback*.

Breakdown or Breakout

The market will develop key levels or patterns that could be in the form of a triangle, channel, wedge, and more. If price breaks higher (from these patterns), we call it a breakout, and if price breaks lower, we call it a breakdown. Just be aware when you go through the setups in the book. Breakouts or breakdowns are the start of a new trend for the market. If you can figure out how to play them quickly, you could be the first to any long move in the market. In the example above, we have two places price broke through, and the subtleties are just in the direction. Simple! The power of a breakout is huge for traders. Coincidently, a false breakout is where the stock looks to pass through that arbitrary place but doesn't (fake out). This is the bane of many traders' existence.

Spotting Key Candlesticks

Again I want to make this very clear; playing reversals is risky, and the best traders will always go with the momentum. The best way to go with momentum is to find an opportune place to buy a *pullback*. The good news is *pullbacks*, *consolidations*, and even *reversals* may show themselves in the same way. Meaning for a trader to have confirmation to enter a trade, they are really looking for the same thing. This is going to be a candle similar to the ones above. All of these candles are seen in the situations listed, and actually give traders greater confidence in those situations. These candles share a couple of things in common. One, they all have *wicks* on the top and bottom; the length is not that important. Two, they all have small bodies relative to the size of the *wicks*. These two facts are important because this indicates a battle between the buyers and sellers, most importantly, indecision. This indecision leads to *reversals*, *pullbacks*, and *consolidation*. Again, *consolidation* and *pullbacks* are opportunities to enter trends. In this book, you will see these candles in almost every setup, memorize them, and put them into context.

Recession-Proof Setups
LEVEL 1

Bearish Setup Explained

For *bear markets*, traders will look to target gaps lower. A gap in the market allows traders to play the filling of the gap or reversals before the gap. The criteria for this setup is simple; you just need to identify a gap, and a stock that is heading towards it. The goal is for the stock to break the first horizontal *support* line that initiates the gap fill. Once that line is broken, the gap fill can happen relatively quickly, and that is where traders can profit.

Why it works

Gaps are formed by the stock being moved during the pre market or after market hours. The reason for these movements could be related to earnings, news, or some other catalyst. When the market opens the very next day, this can produce a gap between the *close* of the previous day and the open of the current day. *Gaps* are places with no buyers or sellers (during market hours), and when price heads towards a gap, it will move very quickly through it because of that fact. Simply put, if no buying or selling happened before at those levels, why would it happen in the future.

Warnings

In *bear markets*, stocks will gap fill extremely quickly so you have to be prepared to react quickly. This does not work perfectly because sometimes buyers or sellers will defend levels right before the gap begins (top horizontal black line above); in that scenario, it is best to play the failure to fill the gap, which results in a bounce and reversal off the *support* line. More importantly, it is best to wait for *confirmation*, which is when price enters the gap (which can be seen in the picture below at the point labeled "long entry").

Pro Tips

In bear markets, my favorite place to enter is when the stock gap fills, like the example below. Basically, where the market fills the gap and sells off again. The best place to In bear markets, my favorite place to enter is when the stock gap fills, like the example below. Basically, where the market fills the gap and sells off again. The best place to (Bioequity.com) of *gaps* eventually get filled, which tells the power of the gap fill strategy.

Setup Above

This scenario above happens all the time and traders have a very hard time playing it. In *bear markets*, gap downs happen all the time and can lead traders to making dumb decisions. There are really only three good plays to take when this happens that I will explain below.

Short Entries

These entry points are the most important to understand in a *bear market*. There are two optimum places to enter short. Once the stock *gaps*, there will be a moment where traders will wait to see if it fills the gap instantly or continues in the direction of the gap. The black bottom line defines this place. After the first candle forms, traders may take the short side and place their stop loss around the open of that first red candle (*short* entry #1). This scenario plays momentum. Another short entry is where stock fills the gap (listed as "target" above), and then sells off. This can lead to a large bearish trend and sell off.

Long Entries

As you can see above, the black bottom line defines where the gap begins. Once price enters the gap, we usually see a move to the top of the gap. This is where traders will usually take profit.

Stop Losses

The stop loss should be placed below (*long* positions) or above (*short* positions) the bottom black line. The amount traders risk is fully dependent on how much they think they can make.

Where to Take Profit

Traders should look to take profit gradually for the gap and go scenario. When the market gaps lower in a bear market, we will likely see more gapping in the next coming days. That is why it is important to take profit slowly, this allows traders to be a part of the future drops, but also to have profit locked in if the market decides to reverse. The best place to take profit is as momentum slows. This slowing of momentum can be seen by smaller candle bodies and larger wicks, or failure to move lower at the same speed. In the gap and fill scenario, it is best to take profit when the gap fills.

Engulfing Candle Momentum Play

ENGULFING CANDLE

TINY CANDLE

1. TINY CANDLE
2. ENGULFING CANDLE
3. CONTINUATION

ENGULFING CANDLE

CONTINUATION CANDLE

Bearish Setup Explained

In *bear markets*, we see engulfing candles all the time. An engulfing candle is when the market produces a candle where the previous candle is inside the range of the new candle. This candle will 'engulf' the previous candle's body. Think of a Pac-man or Russian nest doll scenario. This is basically the inverse of an inside candle, which is where the market produces a candle where the body is smaller than the previous and inside the range. This will happen very frequently in a bearish market. When we see an engulfing candle, it is very typical that a trend begins and is followed by at least one other candle in the same direction, as seen by the continuation candle above.

MATT GIANNINO

Why it works

The psychology behind the levels a candle develops is precious; for example, the tiny candle (above) has an open and close. They are very important levels for the future. For the next candle to basically smash those levels moving in one direction, that says a lot about who is in charge in the market. This is a powerful move, that is why we see a continuation with it.

Warnings

In a market with no direction or on lower time frames, we see these engulfing candles very often without any continuation. The key to this setup, is to use the highest time frames. For example, an engulfing monthly candle will likely see continuation with the next monthly candle.

Pro-Tips

Traders say bulls take the stairs and bears take the window. This rapid selling will often produce engulfing candles, which makes it very easy to play this setup in a bear market. You may not have to wait for the engulfing candle to close to enter the trade. For example, if the candle has already begun to 'engulf,' and there is still time left, it may be good to play the momentum right away as these candles typically close at the lows. There is no telling when it will stop moving in that one direction, and this just increases your risk to reward. Not to mention that you don't have to figure out when to enter on the next candle. You also avoid the scenario where the stock gaps down, and you completely miss the move.

Where to Enter

There are two places a trader can go *short* in this scenario. As you can see, the red candle completely engulfs the smaller red candle. This momentum should bring us lower fast. The better entry point will be at the end of the engulfing candle or the start of the next candle (entry #2). The riskiest entry is going to be right when the first red candle passes the lows of the previous red candle (entry #1).

Where to Place Stop

For this place, your stop-loss is best no higher than ⅓ the candle body. This gives enough wiggle room not to get *stopped* out prematurely.

Where to Take Profit

In this play it is best to hold until traders see consolidation candles. Long wicks and small bodies, will indicate the trend is slowly dying. When that happens it is best to exit..

MATT GIANNINO

Continuation Off Open

3

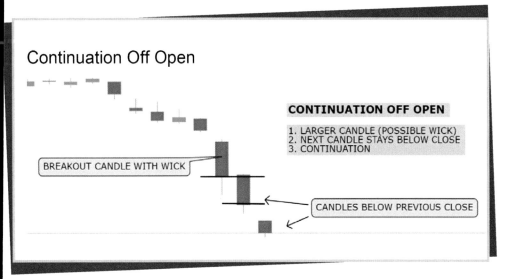

Continuation Off Open

BREAKOUT CANDLE WITH WICK

CONTINUATION OFF OPEN

1. LARGER CANDLE (POSSIBLE WICK)
2. NEXT CANDLE STAYS BELOW CLOSE
3. CONTINUATION

CANDLES BELOW PREVIOUS CLOSE

Bearish Setup Explained

In *bear markets*, trends can begin swiftly with a very large candle (like the first red one above), the trend will likely continue on the very next candle. If the price stays below the *close* (or the black top line drawn above), you will see the momentum continue the very next day. As you can see from the example above, this happens one more time on the next candle, where price stays below the close (or the black bottom line).

Why it works

When a larger candle appears (like the first large red candle), compared to the size of the past candles, it tells us the trend has begun. Like most setups in this book, if traders miss out, they have to grab the *pullback*. This is exactly what the first large candle does before the time ends in the candle; buyers came in and pushed the price up. That was the *pullback* traders were looking for. If this trend is strong and has more steam, the next candle won't explore much higher than the *close* of the previous candle (black top support line above). From there, price should rocket lower for as long as the trend lasts, which is exactly what happens for the very next two candles.

Warnings

The place where the candle closes is key, as drawn by the black lines above. That was the pullback for the trend; therefore, if we see the next candle pop more, it is likely the trend is over or at least losing steam.

Pro-Tips

In a *bear market*, these drops will be large and quick. This just means traders need to act fast and recognize the setup early. Most traders will enter these trades after the breakout candle closes, and place a tight stop with a little wiggle room around the level the previous candle closed. You may get *stopped out* doing this, but if it is a true strong trend, the price will not explore higher. This setup is best used on a larger time frame because it is easier to handle the entry, exit, and stop loss. On smaller time frames, 3 candles can move quickly, and if you aren't strategic your stop loss will get triggered (*stopped out*).

Where to Enter

Once traders find a large bearish candle (with or without a wick), they will then look to enter a trade at the open of the next candle (as indicated by entry #2). This is the best place because the *close* of the previous candle gives traders a defined place to set a stop loss. If the stock ends up gapping lower, this will ruin the risk to reward ratio and make the set up hard to take. Another possible place to enter this setup to avoid gapping is at the close of the first bearish candle (entry #1 risky)

Where to Place Stop

The stop loss should be placed above the *close* of the first bearish candle (or above the open of the entry candle). The amount that traders risk is fully dependent on how much they think they can make.

Where to Take Profit

This play the trailing stop loss works the best. This allows you to ride the momentum; however, far it goes, while locking in profit if it reverses. It is hard to have a defined profit target since the trend could go forever.

Channel Support or Resistance Bounces

4

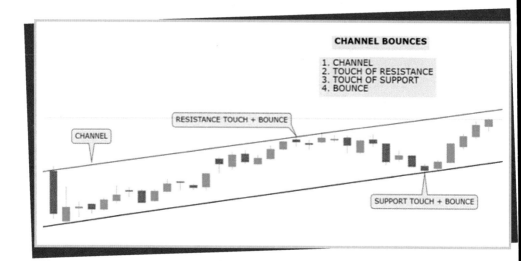

CHANNEL BOUNCES

1. CHANNEL
2. TOUCH OF RESISTANCE
3. TOUCH OF SUPPORT
4. BOUNCE

RESISTANCE TOUCH + BOUNCE

CHANNEL

SUPPORT TOUCH + BOUNCE

Bearish Setup Explained

After consistent selling in *bear markets*, traders will start to see consolidation in the form of a flag, also referred to as a channel. A channel, whether ascending, descending, or flat, is a perfect place for traders to play the *oscillations* in the market. These oscillations are good swing or day trades, but the real money is made if the stock breaks through the channel lower and continues the bearish trend. That is where momentum will pick up and bigger moves will happen. The key to a channel is spotting it as early as you can, to play the up / down movements as many times as possible.

MATT GIANNINO

Why it works

These lines that arbitrarily develop in the market are called supply and demand lines. So whenever prices get close to the *support* (demand) line, we see buyers come in, and likewise, when the price gets to the *resistance* (supply) line, we see sellers come in.

Warnings

The channels work very well initially, but the longer they trade inside the channel, the higher the chance we see a breakout. So your confidence should be high that it will hold in the beginning, which is usually the first 2-3 touches to the *support* and *resistance*. In a truly bearish trend, traders will be waiting for the breakdown lower.

Pro-Tips

The key to drawing a channel as early as possible, in the example above, is to draw the trendline at the first *resistance* (i.e., *resistance* touch+bounce above) and connect it to the prior *resistance*. Then, using the slope of that line, make another trendline connecting to the lowest point of all the candles. The first line will be the top *resistance* line of the channel, and the second line will be the *support* line of the channel. That second trendline would have helped you predict the *support* touch + bounce before it actually happened. Traders never know if a channel will hold, but some key signs are very high or very low relative volume and smaller candles.

Where to Enter

The best place to enter short positions is when price breaks through the channel lower (not pictured above). Another place to enter *short* is touches on the top of the channel (*short* entry). The best place to enter *long* is touches of the bottom (*long* entry). The bottom can easily be defined once we have two touches to the top. Just take a parallel line and attach it to the lowest part of the channel. This will help predict future bottoms before they happen.

Where to Place Stop

The stop loss should be placed below support or above resistance lines. The amount that traders risk is fully dependent on how much they think they can make.

Where to Take Profit

The most common place to take profit for *short* positions is the bottom of the channel (*long* entry + *short* exit) and the top of the channel for *long* positions (*long* exit + *short* entry). It is also common to take profit halfway down the channel.

MATT GIANNINO

Double Top   5

DOUBLE TOP

1. TREND
2. DOUBLE TOP
3. CONTINUATION

DOUBLE TOP

Bearish Setup Explained

In a *bear market* trend, you may see the stock test a level twice. This second test and rejection of this level can lead to a quick sell off, and a new long term bear trend. This second top (double top) is the best time to enter any short positions.

Why it works

The first top *hints* that the sellers are in control by defending that level, but the second top *convinces us* that the sellers are in control. Once we are convinced the sellers have control, we then can be ready for the next big sell off. There is no science behind why stocks top out twice before continuing with the trend. It could be that big banks need more time to sell or many other factors. But the truth is, the double top is a powerful pattern that leads to a strong move.

Warnings

Timing the top of a move is never easy and can lead to a lot of pain. Traders just never know for sure that the resistance level will hold and the double top will form, so be very careful trying to get into a double top too early. It could be best to wait for confirmation, or other evidence to get.

Pro-Tips

The double top could be the highest the stock may be for a long time. Once the top is confirmed and price starts reversing, traders want to be in that trend as quickly as possible.

Where to Enter

The key to entering the double top is waiting for *confirmation* that sellers will defend the previous high made. The red candle (entry) on the double top gives traders *confirmation* of this pattern. The double top can be tricky to enter, and that is why it is important to have evidence it will reverse.

Where to Place Stop

The stop loss should be placed below *support* or above *resistance* lines. The amount that traders risk is fully dependent on how much they think they can make.

Where to Take Profit

Short term traders will take profit at the resistance level of the prior lows (short term exit), and long term traders will let this trade run while scaling out slowly (long term exit).

MACD Sell Signal

6

Bearish Setup Explained

The MACD cross is one of the simplest buy/sell indicator signals, and can really help traders enter sell offs before they happen. The main strategy for playing the MACD is to look for a large trend, followed by consolidation. This consolidation leads the moving averages on the MACD to cross a couple times. Remember, once the fast crosses under the slow that is considered bearish order, and can lead to a new bearish trend. Looking at the example above, the fast crosses the slow twice, but only the second time does it lead to a large sell off. This speaks to the reliability and number of false signals associated with the MACD, aside from that there is power when it does produce sell signals.

MATT GIANNINO

Why it works

Just like one of our other setups, the moving average crossover, this is exactly the same. Just played two moving averages and how they move with one another. When the faster-moving average is on top of the slower, that means we are in a bullish trend, and when the slower moving average is on the top faster, that means we are in a bearish trend. **Warnings:** Indicators historically produce false signals, basically if you took a trade every time these lines crossed, you would be broke tomorrow. Again, this is just another piece of evidence that should be used only if all the right circumstances are met.

Pro-Tips

It only makes sense from a risk to reward standpoint to only trade a clear crossover in the MACD. It is very important to develop a plan for a stop loss because like I said previously the MACD is historic for producing false signals. Also, here are some MACD pro tips. Traders will also only take bullish positions when the two moving averages are above the zero line which is where the histogram flips (basically the middle of the MACD). As well as only take bearish positions when the moving averages are below the zero line. On the chart above, this proves to be 100% true as the stock only moves higher in the bullish trend when it is above the zero line and only moves lower in a bearish trend when it is below the zero line.

Where to Enter

Best *short* entry is when the MACD moving averages cross, fast (blue) goes underneath slow (orange) (entry #1 and #2).

Where to Place Stop

The MACD is hard to figure out where to put the stop loss. But just like the other examples, it can be placed a certain percentage lower than the entry point. The amount that traders risk is fully dependent on how much they think they can make.

Where to Take Profit

The best short term exit is a prior bottom, resistance, or low in the stock (short term exit). The best long term exit for *shorts* is when the MACD's moving averages cross again, fast goes above slow (blue above orange).

Bearish Setup Explained

During a *bear market* trend, the candlesticks will normally only stay within the lower *bollinger band* and the midline. In a real strong trend it will rarely go above the midline. Usually, as the trend weakens, the first real bounce will touch the top *bollinger band* almost perfectly. Once price touches the top *bollinger band* the stock will reverse and continue in the direction of the selling trend. In the example above, this actually takes two attempts before completely reversing. Traders see this time and time again; this is a healthy test of the top of the *bollinger band* and usually leads to a quick sell off and continuation to prior lows as seen in the chart above.

Why it works

As we have seen throughout this book, trends don't reverse instantly. What they normally do is *pullback* and then continue in the direction of the initial trend, or possibly start consolidating. As traders, we are just looking for the right place to enter these trends, and this type of *pullback* is most likely gold. The reason the stock consistently bounces off the top *bollinger band* on the first big bounce is that *bollinger bands* represent where the price can possibly go at any given moment. It expands and contracts due to volatility. From past price movements, *bollinger bands* attempt to predict future price movements, although it is not always 100% accurate it gives us a visual idea of how far price can travel. So once we get that *pullback* to the top *bollinger band*, that is the extent of how far price could have traveled up. In theory, it is the best place to enter for sell off and continuation in the trend.

Warnings

On any *pullback*, it can be dangerous entering. It is just hard to know if it is actually the top when the stock touches the top *bollinger band*. As you can see in the example above, the stock first touched the top *bollinger band* and sold off. Then, went right back to touch the top bollinger band again. If you shorted on the first touch and expected to ride a long term sell off, you would be shocked to see how short the trend actually was. This is because it is hard to know when consolidation is over. Be patient; it pays!

Pro-Tips

The safest way to play this move is to wait for actual *confirmation* that the stock has topped and is heading to the mid *bollinger band*. The evidence for this bottom could be irregular volume, a gap down the next day, indicator *confirmation*, a certain candlestick pattern, candlesticks with wicks, or more. The trick to playing *pullbacks* is placing a stop loss at the highest part of the move, with some wiggle room.

MATT GIANNINO

Where to Enter

This can be a tricky setup to enter because traders need confirmation that the stock will reject the top bollinger band. There are two touches to the top bollinger band where the trader could have entered without getting stopped out.

Where to Place Stop

The stop loss should be placed below *support* or above *resistance* lines. The amount traders risk is fully dependent on how much they think they can make.

Where to Take Profit

The best short-term target is the mid *bollinger band* or the 50% *retracement* of the prior move. The long-term target would be a continuation of the trend until it gets weak. In the example above, a trader could have played the move from the top bollinger band to the middle moving average twice.

High Volume Node Profit Zone

8

HIGH VOLUME NODE MOVE
1. TREND
2. HIGH VOLUME NODE
3. PROFIT ZONE

TREND

HIGH VOLUME NODE

PROFIT ZONE

Bearish Setup Explained

On the right side of the chart you may see a possible mountain range. The peaks are called high volume nodes, which also look like bell shaped curves. High volume nodes are places for *support/resistance* as well as good places to use for profit zones. In the setup above, the stock has the potential to make a run higher, but will quickly run into the high volume node. At this point, it is smart to use this place to take profit, as it requires tremendous volume to move through this zone. Looking at the example above, if we are in a bearish market that is consistently falling, traders will target a high volume node as a place to take profit.

MATT GIANNINO

Why it works

Volume profiles, which are depicted above, show volume from a horizontal point of view. All this tells traders is how much volume is bought at every price level. It is quite a genius. In theory, if a lot of volumes were bought at a certain price (let's say $61), then buyers and sellers will come back to that level to defend it. The larger the volume profile bar goes out, the more volume that was traded there, meaning the harder it will be to break through it. In the real world, this could be similar to the fact that avocados are either $1.00 or $2.00. Nobody wants to sell or buy avocados for $1.50, but the two previous prices produce a lot more buying and selling for some reason.

Warnings

A high volume node is a bell-shaped curve, and at the peak, the highest volume bar is usually the best place for *resistance* or *support*. As you can see above, the rounded bell-shaped curve that is a high volume node makes this idea of *resistance* or *support* vague. The worst part is, if you zoom in on the screen or out, the high volume node will completely change. This, unfortunately, is a very general zone where we don't know exactly where the price will stop. When price moves towards the high volume node it may not exactly touch the highest volume profile, it could stop short or move through it slightly before reversing. This is the one big problem with this indicator.

Pro-Tips

These are great for getting more details on a current trade but not great for planning trades. Like I said before, it is really hard to predict how the price will react around these zones. If you are already in a trade, it may give you extra evidence to know why the price is pausing or why it is moving fast. The best traders will make a note of these levels but not be married to them. These also can be used on every single candle as important levels for day traders, but I don't have nearly enough pages in this book to explain that.

Where to Enter

High volume nodes provide traders with excellent places to enter trades. If the price is below the high volume node, it will be a good *short* entry and above will be a good *long* entry.

Where to Place Stop

The stop loss should be placed below support or above resistance lines. The amount that traders risk is fully dependent on how much they think they can make.

Where to Take Profit

After traders enter a trend, they will look to take profit at the peak of a high volume node (defined by the lines above).

Triple Top Resistance Rejection

9

Bearish Setup Explained

In *bear markets*, the stock may consolidate and produce a defined resistance level. When we have a predefined *resistance* level from the past, it tends to be huge *resistance* or *support* for the future. As we see in the example above, the price touched this level three times, and on the third time, we are presented with a toppy candle. The basis of a toppy candle is one with a thin body and *wicks*, especially above the *resistance*. The more candles like this we see at *resistance* or *support*, the better. At this point, we look for rejection and reversal. This last rejection could lead to a continuation of the initial bearish trend. This usually happens because when the sellers can defend a level three times in a row it shows they are ultimately in control.

Why it works

This *resistance* level that was developed in the past gives us evidence where buyers or sellers were interested and most likely will be interested again. For example, this resistance level (in the chart above) was a place where sellers wouldn't let price get above, so they consistently put their sell orders at this level. This can be visually seen by the *wicks*.

Warnings

The more times the price touches a resistance level, the higher chance that it will break through, because eventually sellers dry up if the buyers are stronger. Just like *chopping* a tree, you never know when the tree finally gives out and falls. The same thing with *resistance* and *support* levels, we just don't know when the next touch will push it completely through. The other downside of playing these rejections is that we never know how far it will pull back from the *resistance* or *support*. The typical rule is on the third touch of an important level; we usually see a follow-through that level. So looking at the example above, price did reject it in the short term, but it could very well breakthrough higher later.

Pro-Tips

In bear markets, traders will look for large sell offs after the third rejection of the resistance. This long consolidation will likely be over and removed all the buying pressure.

Where to Enter

Like every setup, where traders try to enter at resistance or support, it is important to wait for confirmation. In the example, above this can be seen by the thin bodied candle with wicks on the right (entry). The candle with the arrow pointing left just produces a small wick above the resistance line, which confirms it. After seeing that, it would be more than enough evidence to enter the trade at the double top.

Where to Place Stop

The stop loss should be placed below *support* or above *resistance* lines. The amount that traders risk is fully dependent on how much they think they can make.

Where to Take Profit

The best short-term exit is the first consolidation zone or 50% *retracement* of the prior move. The mid-term exit is going to be a 100% *retracement* of the preceding move. The long-term exit may be a break to new lows and a continuation of the trend.

Failed Moving Average Breakthrough

10

MA SLOPING DOWN

CANDLE WITH WICK

FAILED MA BREAKTHROUGH

1. MA SLOPING DOWN
2. CANDLE WITH WICK

CONTINUATION

Bearish Setup Explained

In *bear markets*, there will likely be aggressive sell offs that will lead to big bounces. When we see a moving average that is sloping downwards with a trend in the market, any *bounce* through the moving average will most likely fail. Looking at the picture above, at one point, the candle had a full green body that cut right through the moving average. This usually doesn't last; at this moment, traders will likely play the reversal as the candle usually closes below moving averages sloping down. Like the example above, as we see the wick form above the moving average and the candle body below the moving average. Bodies always mean more than wicks.

MATT GIANNINO

Why it works

We see this all the time in the market, the stock is trending in a direction and makes a *pullback* to a fast-moving average sloping straight down. During these *pullback* times, the reversal rarely lasts long. This is because of two factors, first, the price cannot easily cut through a moving average sloping straight down, second, for stock to truly reverse the fast-moving average generally needs to be flat or sloping down.

Warnings

Not much to say here, this goes with the universal saying, "Don't fight the tape." So if you are trying to go against the trend, that fast-moving average may smack your bank account.

Pro-Tips

These are great opportunities to get into and play the long term bearish trend. These *pullbacks* to the ten moving average end up being the "coulda, shoulda, woulda" scenarios. Meaning you might look back ten days later and wish you got in.

Where to Enter

The best place to enter is at the break of the fast moving average because price generally doesn't stay above (entry #1). When the candlestick closes below the moving average, this will offer traders a safer place to enter, which will be during the very next candle (entry #2). In the example above, traders would have missed a large gap down by waiting till the next candle (entry #2) which makes the safer entry point less ideal.

Where to Place Stop

The stop loss should be placed below the moving average. The amount that traders risk is fully dependent on how much they think they can make.

Where to Take Profit

This setup is best for day traders as they can play the reversal quickly. Profit should be taken at the short term exit, while long-term traders can look to hold for a continuation of the trend, or exit with price crosses back through the ten moving average.

Pennant Pullback Breakout   11

WEDGE BREAKOUT CRITERIA
1. INITIAL TREND
2. PENNANT + MOVE TOWARDS APEX
3. BREAKOUT + CONTINUATION

PENNANT

APEX

BREAKOUT AND RETEST

TREND

CONTINUATION

Bearish Setup Explained

After a bear market trend is initiated, there is a huge possibility of a *pullback/consolidation* in that trend. This may come in the form of a pennant. As price chops through the defined *support* and *resistance*, we get to a special point called the apex, and this is most likely where we see the breakout and continuation with the trend. As seen in the example above. Sometimes, after price breaks out, it may actually retest and reject the resistance of the wedge. This will lead to the best entry point and a big selloff.

Why it works

During every trend, it is very healthy for the stock to *pullback*. During these *pullback* moments, the range gets smaller and smaller, until the apex of the wedge. At this moment, the market just might have removed all the buyers with multiple *pullbacks* and will be able to move lower. This breakout move from the wedge means the trend has fully begun again because all the buying pressure has been removed.

Warnings

At the apex of this pattern, a move can theoretically happen in either direction. We cannot always assume a breakout in the direction of the trend. So don't be married to your plan and instead react to the situation.

Pro-Tips

In a *bear market*, the best move for traders is to wait until consolidation is over and the breakout occurs. This will produce the largest move and lead to the most profits. When the breakout lower happens, most traders will take profit in the middle of the pennant range or the ultimate low of the initial trend. This is because after consolidating for so long, it is very uncommon for the market to make new lows instantly. The *consolidation* and breakout could just lead to more *consolidation* on the macro level.

Where to Enter

This setup can be entered on the *resistance* touch (risky entries). The only problem is traders cannot expect a breakout, and sometimes waiting can provide the best entry point (entry #1).

Where to Place Stop

The stop loss should be placed below *support* or above *resistance* lines. The amount that traders risk is fully dependent on how much they think they can make.

Where to Take Profit

The best short-term exit is the first *consolidation* zone or 50% *retracement* of the prior move. The mid-term exit is going to be a 100% *retracement* of the preceding move. The long-term exit may be a break to new highs and a continuation of the trend.

Moving Average Crossover
12

MOVING AVERAGE CROSS-OVER
1. SLOW MA
2. FAST MA
3. TREND
4. CROSS
5. RETEST AND REJECT
6. NEW TREND

Bearish Setup Explained

After a *bearish market* trend, the market will tend to pull back a healthy amount, and during these times, it may be easy to play the small upward trend with a simple moving average crossover. As you can see in the chart above, we have two moving averages, the fast and slow moving average. This could be the 10 MA (moving average) and 50 MA, or the 50 MA and the 200 MA. After the trend comes to an end, the fast-moving average will cross the slow moving average, producing a buy signal. After crossing, more often than not, the market will pop and head into a new short term trend. If you are lucky and didn't enter the trade of the moving average crossover, you will be presented with a golden opportunity to enter the retest and rejection of the moving averages. These new trends may not last long; that is why it is important to scale out quickly. In a *bear market*, this consolidation will likely lead to a continuation in the bear trend, which will begin when the moving averages cross again (fast under slow). This is the most ideal place for traders to pick up short positions in the market.

Why it works

Stocks that are trending in one direction typically have moving averages ordered from slowest to fastest(top to bottom) for bearish trends like the example above. But once the slow moving average is underneath the fast-moving average (crossover), now they are stacked for a bullish trend. Moving averages, in general, are *resistance* or *support*, so in the example above, once the price goes above the moving averages after the crossover, they acted as a *support*. With the fact that they were stacked in a bullish way, it gives us a high probability of seeing the new trend begin for the time being until they cross again.

Warnings

Moving average crossovers do not always produce a new trend that is easy to profit from. The crossover may also happen late, meaning the new short term trend may have ended after the signal. Moving averages of all sorts cross every single minute in the market, and if you played them all, you might go broke. Be selective and experiment before jumping on this setup.

Pro-Tips

The key to playing the moving average crossover correctly is to look for a steep trend. The steeper the trend, the more likely the pullback will produce an exciting enough move.

Where to Enter

There are three great places to enter this setup. The first being, once price crosses the ten moving average (*short* entry #1 and #2). The second being, the slow and fast-moving averages cross (*short* entry #3). The third, which doesn't always happen, being the retest and rejection of the moving averages above (*short* entry #4).

Where to Place Stop

The stop loss should be placed above moving average lines. The amount that traders risk is fully dependent on how much they think they can make.

Where to Take Profit

The way traders got in could be the way they get out! Either when the price goes above the ten moving average, when the slow and fast-moving averages cross, or when price retests or rejects the moving averages.

MATT GIANNINO

Support or Resistance Level Break and Retest

13

SUPPORT BREAKS

RETEST+ REJECT = PERFECT ENTRY

SUPPORT HOLDS

CONTINUATION OF TREND

SUPPORT/RESISTANCE LEVEL BREAK+RETEST

1. BREAK OF SUPPORT / RESISTANCE
2. RETEST OF SUPPORT / RESISTANCE
3. CONTINUATION OF TREND

Bearish Setup Explained

In a *bear market*, breaking of support levels are key places for traders to get into trends. When the market produces defined *support* and *resistance* levels, it may break and allow profiting from the new trend. As you can see from the example above, the *support* level was defined as it held the price at two separate points. Then all of a sudden, price breaks through the *support* level and doesn't fall much. This is because new trends take time. So the market ends up retesting the new *resistance* level, and at this point, it rejects it. This is the best place to enter any trade. It is at a retest and reject of a predefined level. From there, it continues to lower fast.

Why it works

New trends take a while to develop, especially after breaking a key level, big moves don't always happen instantly. This is very normal after the market has been tight and consolidating for a long time. The market needs time to weed out the buying pressure, turn moving average down, or several other random reasons. We really don't know exactly why these changes in direction take time.

Warnings

When playing breakouts of key levels, you will run into a headache of false breakouts. This is where the market moves through *support* or *resistance*, but it doesn't last long. Very similar to the first breakthrough, the *support* line. As we see above, if the price at the retest+reject zone went higher and never dropped, this would be a classic false breakout. One of the most aggravating moves that can happen to any trader. This is always the risk of playing breakouts. That is why it is key to keep a stop loss on a reversal back through the *support* or *resistance* level.

Pro-Tips

The best place to enter these setups is to get as close as possible to the *support/resistance* level and keep a firm stop a little higher than it. Just like the chart above, at the retest+reject zone, you could enter a short position and put your stop loss in a small amount above the *resistance* line. This just setups traders up to be a part of the move and help them to get out if a false breakout is going to happen.

Where to Enter

There are two great places to enter this setup. The first being, once price crosses the *resistance* level (entry #1). The second, which doesn't always happen, being the retest and rejection of the *resistance* level (entry #2).

Where to Place Stop

The stop loss should be placed below support or above *resistance* lines. The amount that traders risk is fully dependent on how much they think they can make.

Where to Take Profit

The best short-term exit is the first consolidation zone or 50% *retracement* of the prior move. The mid-term exit is going to be a 100% *retracement* of the preceding move. The long-term exit may be a break to new highs and a continuation of the trend.

Head and Shoulders

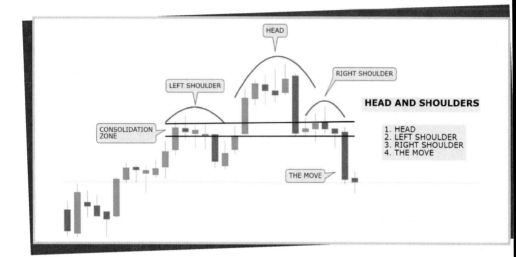

14

Bearish Setup Explained

The head and shoulders pattern above is where we see weakness and eventually breakdown lower. The left shoulder is formed by consolidating and followed by a breakout higher and more *consolidation*. The next *consolidation* level is considered the head. At this point, for whatever reason, the stock may do the reverse of what happened initially. Which drops to the previous *consolidation* range (left shoulder), bounce around some more (right shoulder), and then make one last drop. The last drop is the most predictable and where traders can enter and profit.

Why it works

The first two pops and followed by consolidations (left shoulder and head) above are very bullish. But when the market drops back down to the left shoulder region, a new trend has begun. If the trend were truly bullish, there would be no need to explore lower, just the act of dropping means the trend is likely dead. Now at the right shoulder, the sellers can't move through past *consolidation* levels very easily. What we see is a pause right at the same level as the left shoulder. This *consolidation* lasts just as long as the left shoulder, and we usually see a drop shortly after. This is a highly predictable pattern.

Warnings

This pattern is very hard to spot, and even if you do, you may get chopped out before the move. For example, in the right shoulder above, we see the price go above or below the *consolidation* zone (2 black lines). During this *choppy* action, we get faked out both ways, and if you put your stop loss to close, you most likely will take an early loss in a winning play.

Pro-Tips

Look towards the left shoulder to know where to put your stop-loss, look to see how large the false breakouts were (candle *wicks*), this will help you avoid getting stopped out. Mainly by increasing your stop loss above those previous candle *wicks* on the left shoulder.

Where to Enter

The risky place to enter this setup is at the *consolidation* zone at resistance (entry #1). The safer place to enter this setup is at the breakdown of the *consolidation* zone (entry #2). The best place to enter, which isn't always given, is a retest and rejection of the breakout zone (entry #3).

Where to Place Stop

The stop loss should be placed below support or above resistance lines. The amount that traders risk is fully dependent on how much they think they can make.

Where to Take Profit

In the example above, the stock makes new lows after breaking down, which makes it hard to know where to take profit. The place strategy for taking profit is slowly while dropping or using a trailing stop loss.

3 Bar Play

15

Bearish Setup Explained

This setup is very simple and just involves 3 bars (candlesticks). The first candlestick is called the igniting bar because it ignites the trend. This candlestick should have a larger body than most previous candlesticks. The very next candle is a gift to all traders; this is a *consolidation* candle or called the baby bar. If the range of the baby bar stays below the bottom third of the range of the igniting bar, this will setup perfectly for a continuation with the confirmation candle. The baby bar is a gift to all traders. This gives traders a defined level to put their stop loss (at the *close*) and the ability to enter on the trade on the next candle as long as it stays below the *close* of the previous candle. As traders enter on the third candle, all they can do is hope not to get *stopped out* and for a continuation of the trend. There are also two possible places to enter on the third candle, one is at the open and hope for a run-up instantly, and two is at a break of the highs of the previous two candles. If all criteria are met with the first two candles, the chances are likely it will continue.

Why it works

This is in line with everything we have learned thus far in the book. Trends begin, and traders look for *pullbacks* to get in. The three-bar play is the perfect setup to do just so. The main reason it works is that the igniting candle has a longer body than the previous candles and may have volume accompanying it. It also works because the *pullback* or consolidation with the baby bar is a very tight range, which shouldn't travel much lower than one third the size of the igniting candle. *Pullbacks* in large moves are completely normal, expected, and healthy. The key is that the next candle holds the lows of the baby bar, and breaks the lows of the baby bar. This is called an engulfing candle, which we learned about earlier in the book. Again, engulfing candles indicate complete strength in the trend. This makes the 3 bar play, one of the easiest plays for new traders.

Warnings

This is a tough setup because every detail has to be in place for it to work out perfectly. Traders have to be aware of the volume as well because an igniting bar without volume is meaningless. The volume will confirm this move and will sustain it long term.

Pro-Tips

This is a play for a quick profit; most traders will take profit at the end of the confirmation candle. The trend will only last if there is a sustained or building volume, as well as new highs.

Where to Enter

The best place to enter this setup is on the third candle after the highs are broken from the two previous candles (entry #1).

Where to Place Stop

The stop loss should be placed below the low of the baby bar. The amount that traders risk is fully dependent on how much they think they can make.

Where to Take Profit

The three-bar play is typically a quick move, which is very helpful for day traders. Although you can ride out this momentum for the longer move, it is typically best for traders before the close of the confirmation candle.

Flat Moving Average Magnets

16

EXTREME MOVE

FLAT MAs

EXTREME MOVE

FLAT MA MAGNETS

1. MULTIPLE FLAT MAs
2. EXTREME MOVE
3. REVERSAL

Bearish Setup Explained

In a *bear market*, traders will see consolidation periods where the moving averages constantly cross each other. At the end of this consolidation period, there is a high chance a new bearish trend can begin. Again, once consolidation ends the larger move will proceed. When you have multiple moving averages on the chart, and those moving averages are all flat/close to each other, extreme moves will likely fall back to the middle of the moving averages. During these times, it is best to play the highs/lows for this trading range or possibly think of selling options.

Why it works

Moving averages represent an average of price, and if they are becoming flat, that means there is no direction in the market. There is this concept of mean reversion, which is basically price reverting to the mean, or the moving averages. In the example above, because there are so many moving averages all together, it is really difficult to produce a long term move. During these times, we only end up seeing reversions from the extremes of the range to the moving averages (middle of the range). This can happen for a long time until the moving averages get closer and closer together, then we see a much larger move (similar to recession-proof setup #30). The only way to kick start a new trend is with news or a catalyst.

Warnings

This set up represents a *choppy* (directionless) market, so be careful trading the chop. It is very easy getting stopped out, and you are a slave to any news completely destroying your plan.

Pro-Tips

Try to add another piece of evidence to understand what is happening; this could be volume, trendlines, *divergence*, or more. This type of market can be very random; that is why it is important to stack more evidence.

Where to Enter

Once traders see an extreme move away from the moving averages, it is best to enter after a bottoming candle (as talked about in *"Spotting Key Candlesticks"*). For example, when the price dropped under the ALL moving averages (*long* entry #1), we start seeing candles with thin bodies and long wicks. This indicates the momentum is dying and allows traders to play the move back through the moving averages. The *short* entries are above ALL the flat moving averages, and are followed by a large red candle to confirm the reversal (*short* entry #1 and 2). The *long* entries are below ALL the flat moving averages, and are followed by a large green candle to confirm the reversal (*long* entry #1 and 2).

Where to Place Stop

Entering positions in this setup can be vague and not easily defined, our stop loss has to be the same. The amount that traders risk is fully dependent on how much they think they can make.

Where to Take Profit

This is a great setup for short term traders because of the *choppiness*. Movements don't typically last long, and it's hard to tell where price will go. There is no obvious place to take profit in this setup. Traders can take profit when price crosses one, two, or three moving averages. The more moving averages it crosses the longer a trader may need to hold.

Channel Breakdown and Retest

17

CHANNEL BREAKDOWN + RETEST

1. CHANNEL
2. BREAKDOWN
3. RETEST
4. DROP

RETEST

BREAKDOWN

DROP

CHANNEL

Bearish Setup Explained

In *bear markets*, consolidation can come in the form of a channel or flag. Breakouts from this pattern are highly lucrative for traders, because they generally start a new long term bearish trend. In an ascending channel, we sometimes see exhaustion, which would be in the form of *lower highs* until we breakdown lower from the channel. As you can see in the example above, the first breakdown didn't start the bearish trend, but the retest + rejection of the channel was the beginning of a long term sell-off. Traders can make money on the initial channel breakdown, but it is always safer from a risk to reward standpoint to enter on the next sell off (channel retest+rejection).

Why it works

Channels represent two lines where buyers and sellers have historically defended. For the bottom channel *support* line to give out, that means that buyers are no longer interested and have stopped defending it. Now that buyers are weak, the sellers basically have full control. Like we said earlier in this book, it takes a while for the trend to reverse, and because of this, we usually see breakouts or breakdowns followed by *chopping*. This is healthy and offers traders an ideal entry point. Which is when price touches the channel *resistance* line (bottom black line) and rejects it. This will ignite a large sell off and give traders the ideal place for entry.

Warnings

This retest may never happen, meaning the first move outside the channel may be the only opportunity to enter.

Pro-Tips

Don't ever try to predict moves outside of the channel; just try and react when they happen. More often than not, the price stays inside the channel for extended periods.

Where to Enter

The risky entry point is going to be at a channel resistance touch (entry #1). This is considered risky because it hasn't really broken from the channel, and the move lower would not be as large as the breakout move. The best place to enter this setup is a the break of the channel (entry #2). A safer entry, that doesn't always provide itself to traders, is the retest/rejection of the channel, which is not seen in the example above.

Where to Place Stop

The stop loss should be placed below the channel *support* line. The amount that traders risk is fully dependent on how much they think they can make.

Where to Take Profit

The best short-term exit is the first *consolidation* zone or 50% *retracement* of the prior move. The mid-term exit is going to be a 100% *retracement* of the preceding move. The long-term exit may be a break to new highs and a continuation of the trend.

Recession-Bottoming Setups

Why Bottoming Patterns?

These patterns are important for recognizing the end of the bear market or recession. This book does not talk about reversals as we try to play momentum, but these patterns are hugely important for traders. Knowing when the bear market is over could produce huge opportunities to long term investors and traders, and these patterns can easily tell us when the selling is done. It is completely dangerous "calling the bottom." By using these patterns sparingly and only on the largest time frames, traders will have the best chance of actually predicting the bottom of the market.

Reversal and 10 Moving Average Curl

18

Bearish Setup Explained

For this setup to work well, we need a strong bearish trend, a bottom of that trend, then a pop above the ten moving average. If the stock gets above the ten moving average and spends enough time above it, the moving average should eventually flatten out and *support* price. At this point, it is the ideal place to enter this trade. We have confirmation of the bottom, we have *support* from the moving average, and ideally, the stock will pop off this quickly.

Why it works

For a strong selling trend in the market, the ten moving average will be sloping down aggressively; the reaction to the bottom of this trend produces a quick move hopefully above the ten moving average. The ten moving average visually shows the trend of the stock in the exact moment. So for it to be sloping down during the whole sell-off, we know the direction is bearish. Once we bottom and see that moving average flatten out, now we have proof the direction is no longer down but flat. Any pop at this point has the possibility of now turning that moving average up and starting a new trend.

Warnings

When the price is sitting on the ten moving average, there will be attempts to drop lower, it is important to have some confidence in pattern and avoid getting *stopped out*. It takes time to shake out the sellers but after that happens, the buyers are free and clear. It can't be said enough that this moving average needs to flatten out, so the price can sit on top of it. Another mistake most traders make is playing the first candle that sits on the moving average, the key is to wait for multiple candles to find *support* there. This just further shows the strength of the buyers weakening the sellers.

Pro-Tips

This reversal play only works well if we have a strong trend. This is because strong trends lead to emotions and especially at the bottom of a trend this could mean a huge reversal very suddenly. That is why this play works so well. This quick reversal puts price above the ten moving average which allows traders to capitalize on the *support* and possible continuation higher. This pop off the ten moving average tends to hit resistance first at the mid *bollinger band*, so the larger the gap between them, the more the possible profit.

MATT GIANNINO

Where to Enter

The best place to enter the moving average curl is when the price starts sitting on the moving average (entry #1). This can be seen by the entry above and it is important to note that it is better to wait for the second or third candle to find support on the moving average.

Where to Place Stop

The stop loss should be placed below the ten moving average (purple line). The amount that traders risk is fully dependent on how much they think they can make.

Where to Take Profit

The best place to take profit is usually based on *bollinger band* levels. The two key levels for this are the mid *bollinger band* (short-term exit) and the upper *bollinger band* (long-term exit). Like previous examples, you could also use 50 or 100% *retracement* levels too.

Copy Cat Candles

19

Bearish Setup Explained

The key to this setup is spotting a trend that involves very long candles. If these candles dropped quickly on the news, this setup works even better. After the drop from these long candles, we will eventually get a bottom. This can be spotted by the bottoming candles referred to by *"Spotting Key Candles"* earlier in the book. This is a prime place to enter for a reversal because just as quickly as the stock dropped is how fast it could go up.

Why it works

The market may drop aggressively due to news, earnings, Trump tweets, or more. During these times, it is quick and emotional, and there is minimal buying and selling. Just like our recession-proof setup #1, the gap fill, there

MATT GIANNINO

is little to no buyers or sellers at previous price levels. This poor *price structure* means there is no reason for buyers/sellers to revisit those levels in the future. Looking at the example above, the two candles that dropped may have no structure to them. We can only confirm this by looking at candle volume, or better yet, *volume profiles*. After bottoming and reversing, the next green candle will match the size of the opposing candle only if the *price structure* was weak. Again, if there was small volume and no structure on the sell-off, this will produce a bull run of the same magnitude because of that. This runs true for the next large candle of the reversal, equalling the size of the candle on the first drop.

Warnings

The key to this working effectively is having that large swift candle move in the market. This ensures a poor *price structure* and lets the reversal move happen to the same size as the opposing candle. If for any reason, there was constant buying and selling as the stock fell, it will be much harder for the stock to rise through these price levels again. The main problem with this setup is that a trader cannot expect a swift big candle reversal every time. Only certain market internals for the stock needs to be met and unfortunately, these are invisible to most unless they can analyze *volume profiles*.

Pro-Tips

There is a chance this setup may actually be a gap down in the stock. For example, this could be a weekly candle and one day during the week the stock gapped down. This gap won't be shown on the weekly candles, but only the daily candles and lower. If it actually was a gap down in the stock, we know for sure there was no buying and selling in the candle body. This means that the reversal candle is very likely to be as large as the opposing candle. When entering this trade, it is important to keep a stop loss at the low bottom; a break below the lows will ruin this setup and result in a continuation of the selling.

Where to Enter

The key for this play is to enter during a breakout (entry #1). When you see a large opposing candle and price enters the range of that candle, traders usually see an equal move. The riskier place to enter is before the copy cat candle develops at some type of *support* from the bottom (entry #2).

Where to Place Stop

The stop loss should be placed below *support* or above *resistance* lines. The amount that traders risk is fully dependent on how much they think they can make.

Where to Take Profit

The best place to take profit is at the top of the body of the previous copy cat candle. This could be the open or the *close* depending on the direction.

Inside Candle Reversal

20

OLD TREND

NEW TREND

INSIDE CANDLE REVERSAL

1. OLD TREND
2. NEW TREND
3. INSIDE CANDLES
4. BREAKOUT CANDLE

BREAKOUT CANDLE

INSIDE CANDLES

Bearish Setup Explained

Inside candles are a great opportunity to play a reversal in a stock. The key to finding this setup is to have a trend slowly die to the point where you see very tiny candles with very tight ranges. The first candle sets the range for the rest to trade within. This is the inside range, and once the stock breaks out from the range, this is where the new trend (reversal) begins. As shown in the chart above.

Why it works

Inside candles at the end of a trend signify a place of *consolidation* and a weakening of the trend. In the example above, the bottom of this trend allows big players to accumulate a large amount of stocks from the hands of the desperate shareholders who lost money. In a bearish trend, this is a place where all hope is lost, but the smart money managers know it's an opportunity of a lifetime. They keep the range small because they are quietly buying, doing it when nobody expects it. If you can recognize it, you can be a part of the breakout.

Warnings

This doesn't necessarily mean a reversal; the trend could always continue after this. That type of pattern would then be referred to as a flag. So always be prepared just to play to break out from the range, don't be married to the direction.

Pro-Tips

The more inside candles you have, the larger the breakout that occurs shortly after. In this example above, we had four inside candles, and the breakout leads to a massive bull run.

Where to Enter

The risky place to enter this setup is a touch of the *support* level of the inside candles (entry #1). The safer entry will be a confirmed breakout from the *consolidation* zone, and this will lead to a large move (entry #2).

Where to Place Stop

The stop loss should be placed below *support* or above *resistance* lines. The amount that traders risk is fully dependent on how much they think they can make.

Where to Take Profit

The best short-term exit is the first *consolidation* zone or 50% *retracement* of the prior move. The mid-term exit is going to be a 100% *retracement* of the preceding move. The long-term exit may be a break to new highs and a continuation of the trend.

Cup and Handle

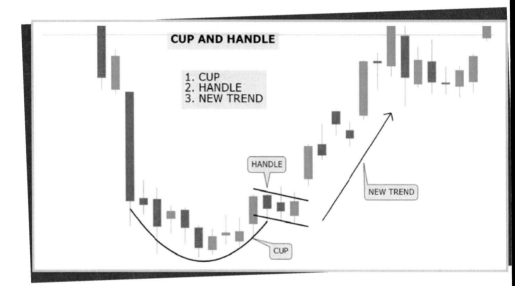

21

CUP AND HANDLE

1. CUP
2. HANDLE
3. NEW TREND

HANDLE

NEW TREND

CUP

Bearish Setup Explained

The cup and handle pattern is a bottoming and reversal play. The criteria for this usually include an initial trend, followed by *consolidation* (in the form of a cup), small breakout higher, followed by a flag(handle), and finally, the start of a new long term trend. This pattern can be tough to spot, but when you do, it can be a very profitable play.

Why it works

The trend slowly dies in the cup portion of this setup. This can be seen by the stock trying to go lower, but each move lower is not as far the drops before. These failed attempts to really drop mean buyers are holding up the stock; this intense battle between the buyers and sellers leads to the reverse. Now the stock

MATT GIANNINO

starts popping, but every drop is higher than the last. This shows the buyers are slowly taking control by moving the stock higher. This brings us to the end of the cup pattern, where the buyers take quick control before the handle. The battle isn't over here because the buyers and sellers go at it again, now producing a handle or a flag. This is seen as a pause in the buying and usually leads to a massive move, which is exactly what happens in the example above. The story of this pattern is basically the slow and methodical battle as the bulls overtake the bears. Victory is shown in the new trend after this pattern.

Warnings

This is a tough pattern to spot in real-time. Not to mention very complex and involves almost a perfect fit of the cup and handle. The key is to try not and force it if the cup and/or handle doesn't look or fit perfectly. It might be best to move on instead of imposing some idea of what will happen to the stock.

Pro-Tips

The larger the cup, the larger the breakout. Most stocks after a severe sell-off will take months to actually bottom. This is fine; this just means that big banks want to accumulate shares at cheap prices quietly. During these long extended bottoms in the market, it will be much easier to chart, spot, and trade this pattern. Traders may never see a handle form on the chart to enter, and that is okay. This setup is very bullish with or without the handle on the chart.

Where to Enter

Traders will look to enter this setup at the upper portion of the cup (entry #1). This will act as *support* and will shortly be followed by the first breakout. The next less risky place to enter is at *support* during the handle *consolidation* (entry #2). This *consolidation* is short and likely followed by the larger move. This *consolidation* will come in the form of a wedge or descending channel.

Where to Place Stop

The stop loss should be placed below the cup support arc (entry #1) or the *consolidation* support line (entry #2). The amount that traders risk is fully dependent on how much they think they can make.

Where to Take Profit

Traders should look to take profit at prior *consolidation* levels for a short-term exit. The best long term exit is at the full *retracement* of the preceding move.

MATT GIANNINO

Recession-Proof Next Steps

Options Basic Course (Free)

Matt has spent most of his trading life mastering options. Options trading allows traders to leverage their small accounts to make some serious profit. Not only that, but long term investors use options to hedge during market 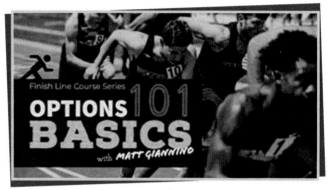 uncertainty. As well as create a passive income by selling options against their positions. Those skills only come after learning the basics, and because Matt believes in the power of options so much, he decided to make this course completely free.

https://www.marketmovesmatt.com/options-basics

Premium Option Alerts (7 Day Free Trial)

Matt mentors, teaches, and gives his best trades to hundreds of options traders every single week. His track record tops most option alert services, and he strives to bring excellence to this group every second. But this group offers so much more. If you decide to take him up on the seven-day free trial, you will receive 3-5 option swing trades a week, 5-10 killer charts, text message alerts, private chat group, unlimited mentorship, two charting live streams, early bird discounted access to all new products, and so much more. Most traders who join never want to leave and on average stay for 4-6 months. If you want your seven days for free click the link below.

https://www.marketmovesmatt.com/trade-alert-special

Market Domination Course

Matt constantly gets phone calls where traders ask to be mentored by him. Although he constantly teaches in his premium group, he has stopped taking one-on-one clients because of a lack of time. This is incredibly tough because Matt wants to get traders to the next level. This is where Market Domination came about, and this is a 100+ video course where you can get every ounce of knowledge from Matt's mind for a fraction of the cost of mentoring sessions.

These 100+ videos take traders through:

- Indicators
- Time frames
- Moving averages
- Charting
- Candlesticks
- Options
- Entering Buy/Sell Orders
- Option spreads
- Fundamental analysis
- Technical analysis
- 10 Expert Trading Strategies
- Long Term Investing Tactics

Market domination is the most thorough trading course on the internet, and the best part is, it comes with **6 months in his options trading group ($936 value for free)**.

https://www.marketmovesmatt.com/market-domination

Disclaimer

NONE OF GIANNINO PRODUCTS AND SERVICES LLC, ITS OWNERS (EXPRESSLY INCLUDING BUT NOT LIMITED), OFFICERS, DIRECTORS, EMPLOYEES, SUBSIDIARIES, AFFILIATES, LICENSORS, SERVICE PROVIDERS, CONTENT PROVIDERS AND AGENTS (ALL COLLECTIVELY HEREINAFTER REFERRED TO AS Giannino Products and Services LLC) AND ARE NOT FINANCIAL ADVISERS AND NOTHING CONTAINED HEREIN IS INTENDED TO BE OR TO BE CONSTRUED AS FINANCIAL ADVICE. "Giannino Products and Services LLC IS NOT AN INVESTMENT ADVISORY SERVICE, IT EXIST FOR EDUCATIONAL PURPOSES ONLY, AND THE MATERIALS AND INFORMATION CONTAINED HEREIN ARE FOR GENERAL INFORMATIONAL PURPOSES ONLY. NONE OF THE INFORMATION PROVIDED IN THE WEBSITE IS INTENDED AS INVESTMENT, TAX, ACCOUNTING OR LEGAL ADVICE, AS AN OFFER OR SOLICITATION OF AN OFFER TO BUY OR SELL, OR AS AN ENDORSEMENT, RECOMMENDATION OR SPONSORSHIP OF ANY COMPANY, PRODUCT OR SERVICE. THE INFORMATION ON THE WEBSITE SHOULD NOT BE RELIED UPON FOR PURPOSES OF TRANSACTING, TRADING OR INVESTING. YOU HEREBY UNDERSTAND AND AGREE THAT Giannino Products and Services LLC, DOES NOT OFFER OR PROVIDE TAX, LEGAL OR INVESTMENT ADVICE AND THAT YOU ARE RESPONSIBLE FOR CONSULTING TAX, LEGAL, DEALERS OR FINANCIAL PROFESSIONALS BEFORE ACTING ON ANY INFORMATION PROVIDED HEREIN." THIS REPORT IS NOT INTENDED AS A PROMOTION OF ANY PARTICULAR PRODUCTS OR INVESTMENTS, AND NEITHER LT NOR ANY OF ITS OFFICERS, DIRECTORS, EMPLOYEES OR REPRESENTATIVES, IN ANY WAY RECOMMENDS OR ENDORSES ANY COMPANY, PRODUCT, INVESTMENT OR OPPORTUNITY WHICH MAY BE DISCUSSED HEREIN. THE EDUCATION AND

Giannino Products and Services LLC does not receive any compensation from any party concerning any stocks or securities mentioned or traded in any of its services.

All content displayed is entirely informational, and is not suggested or intended to replace skilled research, advice or guidance from licensed investors or otherwise.

All information provided is for education purposes only. Giannino Products and Services LLC is not an advisory service or a registered investment broker-dealer. We may hold positions in stocks, options, and other market instruments discussed, but this in no way constitutes investment advice.

All trades and positions posted and/or discussed by the chat room moderator are neither a solicitation to buy or sell a particular security or market instrument, nor are they investment advice.

Giannino Products and Services LLC live trading room, chart examples, webinars, videos, mentoring, emails and any other content on this website is for the sole purpose of education and information, and should not be construed as investment advice. We do not provide tax or legal advice as it relates to stock trading, please refer to a qualified professional for these services.

Trading the markets in any capacity involves substantial risk of loss. This activity may not be appropriate for everyone, and you should only risk what you can afford to lose. Giannino Products and Services LLC does not guarantee trading profits, nor do we guarantee freedom from risk. You must assess the risk of any trade with your broker or financial professional and then make your own independent decisions regarding any trades taken. Giannino Products and Services LLC is in no way responsible or liable for any trader losses whatsoever.

Made in the USA
Las Vegas, NV
23 January 2023

66156616R00062